For Felix   MJH
For Fulvia   RVW

OXFORD
UNIVERSITY PRESS

Great Clarendon Street, Oxford OX2 6DP

Oxford University Press is a department of the University of Oxford.
It furthers the University's objective of excellence in research, scholarship,
and education by publishing worldwide in

Oxford New York

Athens Auckland Bangkok Bogotá Buenos Aires Calcutta
Cape Town Chennai Dar es Salaam Delhi Florence Hong Kong Istanbul
Karachi Kuala Lumpur Madrid Melbourne Mexico City Mumbai
Nairobi Paris São Paulo Singapore Taipei Tokyo Toronto Warsaw

with associated companies in Berlin Ibadan

Oxford is a registered trade mark of Oxford University Press
in the UK and in certain other countries

British Library Cataloguing in Publication Data available

ISBN 0–19–910597–9 (paperback)
ISBN 0–19–910456–5 (hardback)

1 3 5 7 9 10 8 6 4 2

Typeset by Getset (BTS) Ltd
Printed in China

A Song for
Planet
Earth

Text by MEREDITH HOOPER

Illustrated by RUPERT VAN WYK

OXFORD
UNIVERSITY PRESS

This is our place.
One small planet in the vastness of space.
Earth.

Of all the planets the only one
- as far as we know -
to have things that crawl, and swim, and fly,
that creep, and cling, and squeak, and cry.
Things that are born,
    and live,
    and die.

Under the ice in the cold, clear sea,
penguins pirouette,
flying through water.

And streamlined seals
with watchful eyes
search for the holes
where sea meets air.

To breathe.
And rest.

Deep in the leaf litter
down by the roots,
beetles trundle,
lizards scuttle,
fungus spreads.

And a vine sends out shoots,
twisting round tree trunks,
clambering, grasping,
up to the sunlight.
Fighting for space.

Belching, hissing,
scorching hot lava
spills out of the crater,
flows down the mountain,
burying land, burning trees,
choking the living.

But life will come back.
Green things will grow.
Birds will sing again.

Who lives in the woods?
Bear claws scratch the bark.
Deer hooves dent the earth.

And the velvety moose stands in the lake,
four knees hidden,
munching wet weed.

Each has a space.
This is their place.

Fresh green shoots, long strong roots,
the silver of water.

The paddy fields fit between the houses.
Food for the people.

Nothing is wasted
when land is scarce.

Blue-ringed octopus.
Crunching parrotfish.
Purple anemone.
Things that live on a curve of coral.
Soft waving tentacles.
Small hungry mouths.
Sharp stinging spikes.

Eat!
or be eaten!

Tiger, tiger, muscle tight,
dappling shadows, play of light,
on stripy skin and twitching tail.

Tiger, tiger, hiding deep,
watching always how to keep
your cubs alive, and safe, and well.

Tiger, tiger, who can tell
what will happen?

Tiger, tiger, who can know
your enemies?

Nothing moves unless it has to.
Even the ants hide from the sun.

Only the camels walk, on padded feet,
eyelids drooping.

Above the sand an eagle drifts, watching.

Surviving is knowing
where to find water.

Inside houses, cats may doze
eyes half-closed, paws together,
claws furled, tails curled.

But - at night -
cats can see with eyes like torches.

And cats go where they please.
Along the fences,
through the streets,
patrolling, checking.

They know their city.

This smudge in a stone was once a bone
that grew in the jaw
of a dinosaur.

This was yesterday.

There will be tomorrow.

This is our place.
Our small planet in the vastness of space.